MW00813221

Always Be Santa

True Stories From The Guy In The Big Red Suit

Phil Pierce

Copyright © Phil Pierce, 2024

All Rights Reserved

This book is subject to the condition that no part of this book is to be reproduced, transmitted in any form or means; electronic or mechanical, stored in a retrieval system, photocopied, recorded, scanned, or otherwise. Any of these actions require the proper written permission of the author.

Dedication

To my wonderful wife Holly Lynn, my Mrs. Claus, for believing in this book from the very start. She loved Christmas, but loved her family the most.

About the Author

Phil Pierce has been mistaken for the real Santa Claus for as long as he can remember. It's not just that he has appeared as Santa in the movies "A Bad Mom's Christmas" and "Life-Size 2". It might be that he has appeared in commercials, and in music videos. Or that he's made countless visits and appearances to children and families from all over. But it's especially found in the individual moments of magic that occur during his interactions with people, which you'll experience in the wonderful stories that you'll discover in this book. It's also been said that Phil always smells like a Christmas cookie. So there's that too.

Acknowledgment

I would like to express my deepest gratitude to my family for their unwavering support throughout this journey. Thank you for enduring countless revisions with a smile and patience, and for inspiring me to see this through to publication. I would like to acknowledge the extraordinary debt I owe to many people who have helped me along the way. I know that I'll forget someone, so I'll apologize now.

Ken Hawkins was the first person to suggest that I write a Santa book while we sat in the Green Room at The Orange Conference. Coming from a man with his extraordinary history meant a lot to me. Early on I received sage advice from Tim Walker. When I was first outlining the book, Tim had wonderful advice and direction, and put me back on the right path for these stories when I started to stray a bit creatively. I have learned a tremendous amount about the creative process, structure and navigating life from John Alan Turner, Greg Payne, Jon Williams, Liz Hansen and Brandon O'Dell. I also need to include Mike Clear and the staff at Orange for being so supportive of the content we were all creating. Thank you for taking a chance on that "laid back guy " from Southern California, and giving me the chance to be a small part of a very big story. It was an honor to work alongside these amazingly talented writers, creators and friends. I met Lanny Donoho a number of years ago, and at that first meeting he asked me my opinion of a book he was thinking about writing called "God's Blogs". He ended up getting it published. Pick up a copy! Since then I've learned a great deal from him by absorbing his tremendous talent and tapping into his wildly creative brain. When someone makes the comment, "I get that from my dad", it applies here. My dad was the funniest man I ever knew, (and I've known some very funny people) and he was also a great storyteller. My mom was a great writer as well as always being supportive in my creative endeavors. When you've know someone since the 7th grade, you can safely say that you've been through a lot together. No matter what it is, I know that I can always count on Craig Johnson to be there for me. He's not only my best friend, but has been a great sounding board for me as I've gone through the writing process for this book. The wonderful illustrations in this book were created by the brilliantly gifted artist and actor, Brian Bascle. I knew that Brian would do great, but he exceeded my expectations in a major way. I was the best man at Jeff Walling's wedding, but there is so much more to our friendship. Jeff is the author of "Daring To Dance With God" and "Until I Return". Early on in our friendship we discovered our common love for writing and performing. But mostly I'm thankful for Jeff's example as a good Christian man, husband, father and friend. Mr. Phil Perales. "Oh Captain, my captain." He was more than my high school band teacher. Mr. Perales helped me get through that challenging time in my life and taught me about the discipline it takes to refine your talents, and he was very skilled at providing me with timely guidance when I didn't think I needed any.

I would not have been able to get this process completed on time without the support and vision of Joe Wilson and his editing team at AMZ Book Publishing services. This book would not have been possible without the wonderful children and adults who I've been blessed to be able to spend time with during these special connections. Thank you for your kindness, your willingness to share what was on your hearts and for the fun!

Preface

The reason I have titled this book "Always Be Santa" is two-fold. Whenever I share some of my stories on social media, I will close with #alwaysbesanta. That phrase is a reminder to me that when I'm in public, dressed in "civilian" clothes and in everyday situations - there's a chance I'll be perceived as Santa Claus by a child...or an adult. It makes me aware of the need to be on my best behavior at all times. If a child or adult interacts with me as if I were Santa – I need to respond in the best way possible to keep the magic alive.

The other reason behind the title is that sometimes I talk with older kids who have just crossed over into the "non-believer" stage – and they share that with me. I always tell them that it's ok if they don't believe in Santa anymore; they'll just get underwear for Christmas from now on. After I say, "Just kidding" I tell them that I'm ok with them not believing any longer as long as they promise me that they'll always have the spirit of Christmas in their hearts. I also tell them that each of us has a part of Santa inside us, and it comes out when we do our best to treat everyone with kindness, compassion, and understanding and show joy, peace and love as much as possible.

I hope these stories will encourage you to "Always Be Santa", not just at Christmas time – but also all year long.

Table of Contents

Dec. 1st

"The hero is commonly the simplest and obscurest of men."

- Henry David Thoreau.

Sometimes Santa can show up in the most unexpected places. Like the time when I was making a special visit to Nashville, Tennessee. I was at a local grocery store, so I was dressed in "civilian clothes". I wore a red windbreaker that had the name "Santa" embroidered on the left side – and a red/burgundy knit cap. As I turned the corner and went down an aisle, I came upon a group of 4 kids - all around the age of 8 or 9 - standing there with an adult. Their talking stopped immediately when they saw me, and they just stared. I've seen that stare before. It's the "Ok, he looks like Santa – but why would Santa be shopping at our store?" I smiled, waved and said, "Hey you guys." as I walked by and stopped a few feet from them to pick out some snacks. (Not cookies) I overheard one of them say, "Do you think it's really him?" Another commented, "Look at what at the name on his coat!". I found my snacks and moved on, waving to the kids again as I left. Two of them waved back and the other two stared with their mouths open. As I continued to shop, I periodically discovered that this same group of kids were following me. What was very funny was that every time I would spot them, they'd run into each other trying to scatter and hide in different directions. Kind of like Scooby-Do and the gang trying to hide from "a g-g-g-ghost!"

Later as I was waiting to check out, I stood behind a pair of grandparents with their granddaughter of around 7 years old. The little girl would look at me, and then whisper something to her granddaddy. He'd smile, look at me and then answer her quietly. After a moment, he turned to me and said, "Excuse me, sir. My granddaughter was wondering if you're the real Santa. I told her that one sure way to tell is that the real Santa wears a special ring." He glanced down at my right hand and then looked back up and winked at me. You see, on my right-hand ring finger I wear "The Santa Ring"! It has a gold band with a flat face on it. The face has a red background, and in gold are the capital letters "SC". I said to the girl, "Well Becky, your granddaddy is right." She looked up at her granddaddy and whispered, "He knows my name!" I continued, "The real Santa does wear a special ring. And he's the only person in the world that has this ring." I looked around, held my right hand up to her and whispered - "And here it is." She let out an audible gasp. So did Grandmother! She continued to look at it as they checked out. I told her that her granddaddy was part of a special group of people called, the "Secret Society of Ho-Ho Helpers" and that's how he knew about the ring. With wonder she replied, "He is?!" I said, "He sure is! I've known your granddaddy for a long time. Since he was about your age." They all said thank you, and then they were on their way with all of them talking a mile a minute.

As I was loading my grocery bags into the car, the granddaddy approached me and said that he doesn't get to see his granddaughter as much as he'd like because she lives far away. He then thanked me for making him look like a hero to her. I looked at him and said, "Sir, I saw the look in her eyes when she'd look at you. You're already her hero and you always will be." Suddenly we were both at a loss for words, just looking at each other. But there was an understanding. We shook hands, and went our separate ways.

REFLECTION:
I'm glad I took the time to connect with them. It's important, because you never know when you'll be able to give some kids a fun story to tell their friends, or to help a granddaddy have a hero moment with his granddaughter.

-       Who are your heroes, and why?

Dec. 2nd

"The greatest gift you can give another is the purity of your attention."

– Richard Moss.

I made a visit to a company Christmas party for employees and their families at an Ice Complex in Huntsville, AL. It was November, but the temperature in Huntsville when I arrived was 65 degrees. They had use of the entire complex and I was scheduled to be there for 3 hours. It was chilly inside, which was fine with me because it tends to get pretty warm in the big red suit! This company party was a little different than others I've visited because the kids didn't just take a picture with me, tell me what they wanted for Christmas and move on. They had access to me for the entire 3 hours. That led to some great conversations that kept me on my toes. A little girl of about 8 years old kept coming back to talk with me. At one point, she just stood next to me with her head on my shoulder and touching the soft sleeve of my coat as I talked to other kids. When it was just the two of us, she looked up at me and asked, "Santa, do you believe in God?" It was an unexpected question, but I didn't mind. I said, "Of course I do." She then asked, "Do you go to church?" I replied, "I sure do. I try to go every Sunday." She raised her eyebrows and said, "There's a church at The North Pole?!" I chuckled and said, "Well, why wouldn't there be? Going to church is very important to me, Mrs. Claus and the elves." She thought about this for a few seconds. Suddenly her eyes widened, she smiled and asked excitedly, "Santa, will you come to my church tomorrow morning?!" I was very touched by her request and said, "Sweetheart, I would love to visit your church. I'll bet it's very special because you go to it. But I'm afraid I have to go back to The North Pole tonight." She thought again and said, "That's ok Santa. Maybe next time!"

Another little girl who came up to talk to me seemed to be a little concerned about my weight. After we talked about her Christmas Wish List, she patted my tummy and said, "Santa. I think you should try to lose some weight." She wasn't being rude. This sweet girl was just concerned. I laughed and jokingly said, "Hey! I ate a lot of cookies to get this tummy!" She replied, "Do you like salads?" I said, "Yes. I love salads! Especially with cookies sprinkled on it." She said, "You're not helping, you know." "Sorry" I said. She then asked, "If I fixed you a salad, would you eat it? I said, "You bet I would. Don't worry, honey. Santa is very healthy. Mrs. Claus takes very good care of me." That seemed to satisfy her and she was on her way.

REFLECTION:
The things that children have in their hearts and have questions about are very important to them, so they're important to me too. I need to make sure they know that by giving them my full attention and in how I answer them.

-       How important is it to REALLY listen to someone when they're talking to you?

Dec. 3rd

"Just be kind and brave. That's all you ever need to be."

– Mister Rogers.

I had the privilege of visiting with some very sweet and brave kids at a Children's Hospital. It was a very casual visit - well, as casual as it can be when Santa shows up. I got to spend one-on-one time with each of them, and their siblings. I talked about "The Avengers" with one little boy. He was also fascinated with everything I was wearing, and asked questions about who made them. He really liked my belt. It's made of real leather with holly leaves stamped on the top and bottom all the way around, and a very shiny, big brass buckle. I told him that Sherman The Elf made it for me about 100 years ago. So, it was still pretty new in Santa years. Not only was he inquisitive, but he also had a constant smile on his face – so I couldn't help but smile too. I also spoke to the sister of another little girl who was a patient there. When I asked her if there was something special I could bring her this year, she said "All I want for Christmas is for my sister to come home from the hospital." A tear ran down her cheek, and then she buried her face in my chest and held me very tightly. The moment of silence wasn't awkward. She needed a release, I guess.

After wiping the tears from her face with my gloved hand, I told her that I was proud of her, and what an unselfish and loving thing that was to wish for at Christmas. Then...I got a present...a beautiful smile from her. One of the last kids I spoke to had a very sweet smile on her face. She beat me to the punch before I could ask her what she wanted for Christmas and said, "Santa! I already got my Christmas present!" I asked her what it was, and she replied, "I got a new heart!" I told her how happy I was that I got to hear such great news from her, and that she was one of the bravest people I'd ever met.

REFLECTION:

I went to this hospital thinking that I needed to do whatever I could to lift their spirits and let them know that everything was going to be ok. It turned out that they were the ones who lifted me up with their brave, positive attitudes while enduring some very tough circumstances. I left feeling very humbled and blessed that God allowed me to spend time with those wonderful children, and to learn so much from them.

- Share a time when you went to lift someone's spirits, and they ended up doing that for you.

Dec. 4th

"Some of your greatest blessings come with patience."

– William Wiersbe.

I was at a photo studio in Charlotte, North Carolina that was doing Santa pictures. A family with three children came in to have their photo done. The children's names were Ben – age 9, Jack – age 7 and Emily – age 5. Jack came running over and hugged me. Emily climbed up on my lap, and Ben sauntered over at his own pace. After we were done taking pictures and the parents were picking which photos to go with their package, I had time to talk more with the kids. Ben suddenly stated, "Ok. I know that you're just some actor that's pretending to be Santa." Amused, I replied, "An actor?" But I have a real beard." Emily stroked my beard. "And it's really soft too, Ben!" she exclaimed. "Nope. No way." Ben responded. "You're not real." I looked at Jack, then Emily. They were looking up at me in anticipation of my answer. "Well, then how do you explain the fact that I have...the Santa ring!". I held out my hand to reveal the Santa ring that I wear. Emily gasped in wonder. "Ben! He really does have the Santa ring!" Jack joined in. "Do you have dogs at the North Pole?" "Oh, yes. I love dogs!" I said. "How many dogs?" asked Jack. "I'm not exactly sure. Probably about a dozen. It's a big place." I answered. Emily got excited. "What about kitties?" At this point, Ben was pacing back and forth as if he were a juvenile Jack McCoy from "Law & Order". He stopped, turned to face me and asked, "What if no one believed in Christmas anymore? Then what? What would you do?" I thought for a moment, then spoke directly to him. "Ben, that's a very intelligent question. You're a smart young man. But I don't think that there will ever come a time that people will stop believing in the spirit of Christmas." He countered quickly with, "I have friends that don't believe in you...I mean, in Santa anymore." "They're poops!" Emily quickly responded. I said, "Well, what a person chooses to believe in is entirely up to them. But I want you to understand something, Ben. Believing in the spirit of Christmas and believing in Santa are two different things." "I don't understand," Ben replied.

I continued, "The spirit of Christmas is joy, peace and love. That was given to the world at the very first Christmas when Jesus was born. And it's still around today because people choose to continue to believe in it. You see, Santa Claus isn't the cause of Christmas. I didn't create it. I'm just part of it to help spread the spirit of Christmas in any way that I can. And I choose to be a gift giver because God gave us the greatest gift ever on that first Christmas. Now, you can choose not to believe in Santa anymore. Like I said, that's up to you. But there are three things I want you to always believe in. I want you to always believe in yourself, believe in your family and believe in the spirit of Christmas." Ben got quiet and I could tell he was pondering everything I had just said. The stillness was broken by Jack asking. "How long did it take you to build the North Pole?" he asked. Followed by Emily asking, "What are doggies names?" Before I could answer their questions, Ben was pacing again. He was ready for his re-direct. Stay tuned for the rest of the story...

Dec. 5th

"Patience attracts happiness; it brings near that which is far."

– Swahili Proverb.

If you remember from the previous story, Jack had asked me how long it took to build The North Pole and Emily asked about doggie names. I decided to tackle Jack's question before Ben could get started. "Well Jack, we've added on to The North Pole over the years. So, it'll probably never be completely finished. Our last big addition was for making Razor Scooters. But it doesn't take us as long as you'd think to build things like that because at The Pole, we have the ability to move and do things faster than normal when we need to. Jack's "Whoaaa!" was cut short by Ben's follow-up question. "How did you get here today? Your sleigh? I didn't see it outside." Without skipping a beat, I replied, "I drove a Ford Explorer." "Ah-HA!" Ben said, thinking he'd trapped me. I continued. "Ah- ha, what? I'm just being honest with you. Now, think about it. If I flew the sleigh around Charlotte in broad daylight, the magic, mystery and wonderment of Santa's sleigh flying through the night on Christmas Eve would be ruined for a lot of people. My sleigh is one of those things that you don't need to see to believe in. Besides, I don't bring the sleigh I use for the "Big Night" out for special trips like this. I fly a smaller model and only use one reindeer. This time, it's Blitzen. He likes to stay busy by going on this trip with me." "I didn't know that!" said Emily in astonishment.

Ben was still trying to process my unexpected response to his doubting of my mode of transportation when he said sardonically, "Really? Santa drives A Ford Explorer?". I said, "Well, I am today. I left Blitzen and the sleigh with a friend of mine nearby who's a member of a secret group." "What secret group?" Ben asked. I said, "SSHHH". Ben looked around and whispered, "What secret group?" I chuckled and said, "Not SSHHH as in be quiet. SSHHH's in the Secret Society of Ho-Ho Helpers. There are members all over the world. Anyway, my friend let me borrow his car to come here. It's less showy." Ben's demeanor seemed to be changing. Like I said. He was a smart kid, and I was hoping that if I treated his questions with respect and answered them simply and directly– maybe he'd come around. He opened his mouth to say something, but a barrage of questions from Jack and Emily interrupted him. "How old are you?" "Is my daddy on the Nice List?" "How big are elves?" "Do you eat every single cookie on Christmas Eve?"

I think that I did a pretty fair job of answering all of their questions by the time their mom said it was time to go. As Jack and Emily went over to get their coats, I asked Ben to hang back for a minute. What Ben didn't know was that earlier Emily had whispered to me that she didn't think Ben liked her because he picks on her a lot. I spoke quietly to him. "Ya' know, Ben. Being a big brother is a special blessing. And it's also a big responsibility. Part of that responsibility is taking care of little sisters." He glanced back at Emily, then looked at the ground. I continued, "You need to be her protector...her hero, so that she feels safe, and loved and knows that you'll always be there for her." Ben started to protest, but then stopped himself and asked, "How did you know?" I told him that it didn't matter how I knew. What did matter was that I knew I could count on him to make the right choices because he was an awesome young man with a good heart. Emily and Jack had put their coats on and came over to say their goodbyes. Ben left to get his coat. I got hugs from Emily and Jack, and just before she left Emily whispered to me, "Can you please bring my mommy some new slippers and a robe? Something in pink with flowers." I said, "I'll see what I can do. Ok?" "Ok!" she said happily, and off she went. Ben walked over, looking down at his shoes. He stopped in front of me, looked up at me and said, "I believe in you again. Thank you, Santa." We shared a "guy hug", and Ben ran out of the room saying, "Mom! Guess what?!"

REFLECTION:
I'm glad that I didn't dismiss Ben's questions or try to fool him by not answering them directly. I've found that most kids like it when an adult treats their questions or concerns with respect and patience. It seemed to be that way with Ben and he had a change of heart.

- Patience is a virtue, but not always easy. What can you do to be patient with someone who asks a lot of questions, or seems like they're trying to prove you wrong?

Dec. 6th

"There is no small act of kindness. Every compassionate act makes large the world."

– Mary Anne Radmacher.

I love Christmas Tree lighting ceremonies, so I was really happy when I was asked to make an appearance at one for a high-end outdoor shopping and dining center. I got to ride in on a fire truck! Even better, I got to stand in the basket attached to the ladder at the back of the truck – with lights and sirens going! What an awesome entrance! When I stepped down from the fire truck, several families and children greeted me on one side. After saying hello and waving to them, I walked around the front of the truck to the other side and was suddenly swarmed by dozens of kids, with shouts of "Santa!" and warm hugs! I sat in a very ornate chair at the base of the huge newly lit Christmas tree and began posing for pictures with kids and families. One little girl came up and gave me an ornament that she had made the day before. She told me that she wanted to bring me a gift, because I brought gifts to kids all over the world and she wasn't sure if I ever got a Christmas gift. I hugged her and told her that her special gift warmed my heart.

After a while, I had an unexpected visit with an older boy, maybe around 10 years old, who walked up for a picture. He didn't look like he was being forced to do this, but he had an expression on his face that I couldn't figure out. His name was Chuck. I told him how glad I was that he came to talk to me, and that he didn't need to do the "sitting on my lap" thing for the picture. We finally got around to THE question. I asked him what he wanted for Christmas. He told me, but I had to ask him to say it again to make sure I heard him correctly. Chuck said, "I want my Pop back." I asked him what he meant by that. He said that his dad had died a few months ago. I could tell Chuck was trying to be brave, but there was an earnestness in his eyes - which were looking directly into mine. I told him how sorry I was to hear that, and asked him if his dad had been sick for a while. He said yes. I said, "Well, Chuck I feel blessed that you felt like you could share this with me. I know that you miss him terribly, but you know that he's not sick anymore. And that's a great gift for him, isn't it?" Chuck nodded yes. Suddenly it felt like it was only Chuck and me there...just talking. I didn't hear the music, or laughter or anything else going on around us. "Chuck", I continued. "You're a smart young man, so I know you understand that I really can't do anything about bringing your dad back. But what I can give you is hope. Everything will be ok. You have a good heart and you are very brave. That's a gift you got from your dad, isn't it?" He nodded yes again. "Your dad would want you to have a nice Christmas, and it will honor him for you to do that. I know it won't be easy. But I also know that you and your family can do it in your own way. Do you think that's possible?" "Yes Santa", he said. "Well, I believe it. And I believe in you, Chuck. Now, can we do the guy hug? Ya' know, the three pats on the back thing?" He smiled and nodded yes. We hugged, and I patted Chuck three times...he squeezed me. Chuck looked at me and said, "Thank you Santa." I choked out a "Merry Christmas Chuck", and he was on his way.

REFLECTION:
It's hard when you lose a loved one, especially when that first Christmas rolls around. Chuck needed to talk to someone about it, and I'm so happy that he chose Santa. Sometimes it's hard to know what to say to someone who has suffered a loss.

-      What are some things you can say, or do in a situation like that?

Dec. 7th

"Encourage everyone you meet with a smile or compliment. Make them feel better when you leave their presence and they will always be glad to see you coming."

– Joyce Meyer.

I was in town for a special visit, when I stopped at an Italian restaurant for some takeout. I was dressed in "civilian clothes". While I was sitting on a bench in the waiting area waiting for my food, I had this feeling someone was looking at me. I looked around and noticed a young girl of about 7-8 years old looking over at me. She was sitting at a table with her Mom, Dad and older sister. I smiled at her, and after a couple of moments her older sister brought her over and said, "My sister wants to know if you're the real Santa." I looked at the younger girl, who was holding an "Elf On The Shelf", and I said "Well, I see you have one of my..." I clapped my hand over my mouth and looked around. Then I said, "Iiiii mean, I see you have a little elf friend." The girl told me her elf was named Evie. I said, "Well, Evie has had fun being with you and helping me...I mean, helping YOU out." It was time to pay for my food, and I told the girls it was nice talking to them, and they went back to their table. After I paid, I looked over and the little girl was still looking at me. I glanced at the parents and pointed as if to say, "Can I come over?" They smiled and waved me over. I walked over to their table, knelt down on one knee and said quietly to the girl, "Can you keep a secret?". She smiled and shook her head "Yes!". I said, "You know that adults need to have a driver's license to drive a car, right? Well because I fly a sleigh – I also need a sleigh license." I took out my wallet and showed her my Sleigh License and motioned "Shhhh" - then winked at her. She whispered loudly, "I knew it!! I KNEW it!!!", and bounced up and down in her chair. Mom and Dad wanted to see the license too, so I showed them. Mom cupped her hand over her mouth, and Dad said, "Whoa!". I quietly wished them Merry Christmas early, said goodbye to the girls, told Evie the Elf I'd see her soon and left.

REFLECTION:
I'm glad that I didn't just keep to myself while at that restaurant, and simply picked up my food and left. If I had, I would have missed out on a fun encounter.

-        Have you ever had a moment when you had to decide "Should I engage with this person or not?" And you were glad that you did?

Dec. 8th

"I've learned that people will forget what you said, people will forget what you did, but people will never forget how you made them feel."

– Maya Angelou.

You might not think that Santa would appear at a Senior Assisted Living Center Family Christmas Party. But I have been many times. I had a feeling this one particular night was going to be special by the way it started off. As I made my entrance, the singer they'd hired for the party sang "Here Comes Santa Claus" – Sinatra style. "Here comes Santa Claus. Baby, it's Santa Claus." You get the picture. I was then directed to where I'd be sitting for pictures and saw that they had a nice "Reserved for Santa" sign attached to a big, fancy chair next to a beautifully decorated Christmas tree. As I posed for pictures with the residents and their families, I met a sweet lady named Irene who told me that she was 93 years old. (She didn't look 93!)

While we waited for the photographer to get ready she whispered to me, "I want a puppy for Christmas". Naturally, I thought she was being playful and I replied, "Aww. That would be fun, huh? I love dogs." Irene looked at me with a hint of sadness and said, "I've been so lonely for a long time. I'd just like a companion." Before I could respond to that, the photographer said it was time to take the picture. We smiled and took the picture. Irene thanked me and went off to sit down. More pictures with other residents followed, but I couldn't get what Irene had said to me about being lonely off my mind. I was done with the picture taking session, so now I was able to mingle with everyone. The singer, accompanied by a karaoke type system, started singing my favorite Sinatra song - "You Make Me Feel So Young". I walked across the room, held out my hand to Irene and said, "This old Santa would love to dance with a beautiful young lady." She cupped her hand over her mouth, and then took my hand as she smiled shyly and joined me in the middle of the room. We danced – nothing fancy, but we did a good job. I looked at the expression on her face, and it was as if she were transported

17

back to her younger years. Her eyes lit up and she had a beaming smile. We even did a slight dip at the end of the dance. I didn't need a picture of that moment. I'll remember it forever. God bless you, Irene.

REFLECTION:
-     How can you or your family be an encouragement to someone in the situation described in this story?

Dec. 9th

"It is fun to have fun."

– Dr. Suess.

I was at a grocery store near Atlanta once, and found myself on the same aisle as a dad with his son - who was about 6 years old. The dad said to the son, "Matthew, should we get Cheerios or Fruit Loops?" The son said, "Fruit Loops!" The dad did a double take looking at me and said, "Hey. I think I know you from somewhere, but I can't think of where." The son said, "Daddy, I know. It's Santa Claus!" Dad didn't pick up on what his son just said, and I smiled and winked at the son. The dad asked, "Where do you live?" I replied, "The North Pole." He chuckled and said, "That's funny. No, seriously. This is gonna drive me nuts." The son again said, "Daddy! It's...Santa!" The dad continued, "Man! Where have I seen you before?" I calmly said, "Well, maybe on Christmas Eve? You know, delivering presents? Flying reindeer?" I looked at the son for confirmation. He smiled and shook his head. "Yes!" Hoping to finally get through to his dad, the son said "Daddy! Santa...Claus!" and gestured with his arms as if to say, "Hello?!" I said to the dad, "Well, you'll figure it out soon. It was nice seeing you again. Bye Matthew!" The son's eyes got big and he waved. As I walked away I heard Matthew say, "See, daddy! It was Santa!" It's always fun to encourage a child's imagination.

REFLECTION:
-     Describe a time when you've had some spontaneous fun.

Dec. 10th

"The purpose of human life is to serve, and to show compassion and the will to help others."

– Albert Schweitzer.

I was at another Children's Hospital visit, when a couple with a baby girl stopped by for a "Baby's First Christmas" picture. As they handed the girl to me, they told me that she was blind, but that wasn't why she was a patient there. I held her so that she was facing me, and softly said to her, "Hello beautiful". She responded immediately with a big, sweet smile. I started to melt. The smile went away, and I said, "Where did that sweet smile go?" The smile came back, accompanied by a happy sound and then she buried her face in my beard. Her mom said, "Oh my goodness! She never acts like that with strangers!" This continued for a couple of minutes with her alternating between smiling and cooing when I talked to her - to snuggling. Reluctantly, I had to give her back because the line of kids was getting longer. We took a picture, the parents hugged me and thanked me and then they left. After about an hour, I saw the parents with the baby again out of the corner of my eye. The little girl was fussing this time. The parents walked over and apologized for coming back, and shared with me that their daughter had just gone through some tests that involved poking and prodding. I said, "I'd be fussing too!" Then the mom said, "She really took to you before. As you can see she's really unhappy. We were wondering if you'd mind holding her again to see if that helps her." How could I turn that down? I held the baby the same way - facing me. The moment she heard my voice again, she started smiling. After we "talked" a little longer, she laid her head against my chest, snuggled up...and went to sleep. I stood there with this beautiful, sweet child sleeping soundly in my arms and swayed back and forth. I looked over at the parents, who were smiling with their arms around each other. What a wonderful, touching moment.

REFLECTION:
- How can you help others in small or big ways?

Dec. 11th

"Laughter is timeless. Imagination has no age. And dreams are forever."

– Walt Disney.

I was in a bookstore the other day and was dressed in "civilian clothing". As I do often, I was wearing my Santa Claus ring, and my watch that looks exactly like the one used in "The Santa Clause 2" movie. A mom and her two kids - a daughter about 6 years old and a son about 9 - ended up in the same aisle as me. The girl looked at me, and I smiled back. She gasped and said, "Santa! Hi!" I said hi to her, and the brother was looking at me like some 9-year-old boys might look at Santa. The mom just stood there with her mouth open. The little girl asked me what I was doing here, and I told her that I was visiting some friends of mine and decided to stop by and get some books. I also told her that I was so glad to see that she was getting some books to read. The older brother said, "You're not the real Santa!". To which his sister replied emphatically, "He is too!" The brother countered with, "Pffft. Well, I don't believe in Santa anymore." The little girl looked at me with eyes that said, "Oh no! I hope that my brother didn't hurt your feelings!". I smiled and winked at her, and said to the brother the same thing I've said to others who have made that same comment to me. I said, "That's ok that you don't believe in me. God allows us to make our own choices about everything. But, I believe in you." For a brief moment, he had a look in his eyes of, "He believes in ME?" Then I took out two of my Nice List cards and said, "But how do you explain that I knew that I was going to see both of you, so I made sure to bring you these two Nice List cards? Because, you're both on the Nice List! That's why!" The sister stared at the cards and started tearing up. So did the mom. Then the mom said, "Santa? Is there one for me too?" I replied, "Well, of course there is my dear. You're the hero. Where else would these two have received the example for getting on the Nice List?" I handed out the cards, and the little girl saw my SC ring. I explained what it was, and while they looked at it, the brother asked, "So "Santa", where's your sleigh? On the roof?" I said, "Well now, if I flew my sleigh into town during broad daylight, that would cause quite a commotion huh? Oh, by the way – when I make these quick trips I don't use the big sleigh that I fly on Christmas Eve. I use a much smaller sleigh that only needs one reindeer to fly it. This time I brought Blitzen with me. He likes to make these little trips."

At this point I have the attention of not only the brother, but the little girl and mom too. "Anyway, there is a place right outside of town that lets me land my sleigh there. Kind of a secret, stealth thing." The brother now had a look on his face as if to say, "Wait. This is kind of making sense." He then asked, "Then how did you get here?" I said, the guy that owns the place where I landed the sleigh let me use his car. Again, I can't fly the sleigh in town." He looked at me as if to say, "I... I've got nothin'." Mom said, "Yes!" to herself. The little girl hugged me tight and said, "I love you Santa!" I told her that I loved her too, then said to the brother - who was dumbstruck - "Hey, let's just keep it between us for now. Let's do the guy 'fist bump' and then we'll go from there. Deal?" Eyes wide, he shook his head "Yes" and we fist bumped.

REFLECTION:
Sometimes kids, and adults, repeat the things they've heard from friends or family members as they are trying to form their own opinions or beliefs.
-      How have you handled someone who believes differently than you about something?

Dec. 12th

"Life is made of all precious moments, all we have to do is celebrate these every day!"

— Purvi Raniga.

I recently had a couple of special encounters with two different autistic boys when they came to have their picture taken with Santa. The first visit was with a boy who was very curious about me. He was so curious that he came back to visit me 3 times in the space of about an hour. He had a very sweet, gentle disposition about him. At times, he would seem fascinated by my beard and mustache and kept touching it and looking at it very closely. Never speaking, but smiling all of the time. As our visit continued, he made himself at home and was ready to just hang out with Santa on the couch by reclining on one of the arm rests. It looked comfortable, so I joined him by reclining on the over one. It made for a great picture!

At the beginning of the visit with the other boy, his parents told me that he doesn't say much and probably wouldn't look at me. During the picture taking and our visit I told him how happy that I was to see him, that he had grown a lot since I saw him last year and I couldn't wait to bring him some special surprises this Christmas. Suddenly, he stood up and turned around to face me...and started singing the chorus to "Jingle Bells'. After his parents and I got over our surprise, we all joined him in singing the song. He finished, hugged me and said, "Bye Santa" and then was on his way.

REFLECTION:

I cherish special moments like these. I didn't do anything extraordinary to cause these boys to engage with me the way that they did. I took their lead and just went with it.

- Have you ever experienced a time when your interaction with someone else exceeded your expectations? What made it special?

Dec. 13th

"It's not how much we give, but how much love we put into giving."

– Mother Teresa.

Today during a lull in picture taking, an older man came up to talk to me. With a warm smile, he asked me if he could tell me a Christmas story. "Of course!" I said. He told me that he served on the front lines with an infantry division during the Korean War. I said, "Thank you very much for your service" and shook his hand. He continued, "It was Christmas Eve 1951 and my squad had returned to base camp. Earlier my mother had sent me a letter telling me that she wanted to send me a box of things for Christmas. She also asked how many men were in my squad, and their names. I sent a letter back telling her that there were 10 other men and gave her the names. At camp, we celebrated Christmas Eve with a fire in the 'fireplace', and a meal of turkey, mashed potatoes and gravy. It being December in Korea, our food wasn't piping hot. But just the smell of all of it made us think of home. Near the end of our meal, someone, and I don't know who it was, started singing 'Silent Night'. One by one we all joined in and made it through the song." He looked off in the distance. I could tell that for a brief moment in his mind, he was right back there at Base Camp. "Anyway, we all went to our racks for a night's sleep. Before I turned in I wanted to see what my mom had sent me. I opened the box and found a box of treats for me...and 10 individual boxes with the names of each soldier in my squad." His eyes began to mist. He cleared his throat and went on. "As everyone else slept, I went to each rack and quietly placed the boxes for each man. When my buddies woke up on Christmas morning, they each found a present with their name on it. And suddenly, 'Home for Christmas' had arrived from thousands of miles away - and now didn't seem so far away". I was glued to every word he told me. Even after all this time, as this man was telling me this story - he got emotional. And I did too. I thanked him for telling me such a wonderful story. We shook hands and he told me that he hadn't shared that story with anyone outside of his family for probably 30 or so years. I am so grateful that he decided to share it with me.

REFLECTION:

His mother understood that a huge part of Christmas is about giving and spreading joy to others. She gave to people that she didn't even know, and it allowed her son to be able to play Santa to some brave soldiers who needed it. It's a gift that her son continues to carry with him in his heart to this day.

- What are some small, quiet ways to not only give to people that you know, but to those that you don't know?

Dec. 14th

"The wonderful thing about joy is sharing it with others."

– Anonymous.

Whenever I'm driving during the holidays, I keep a Christmas stocking with candy canes in it on the passenger seat of my car for special encounters when I'm out. One night, I had just finished taking Santa photos at a big shopping and entertainment center in a very busy part of Los Angeles. I had just turned from 3rd street onto La Brea Avenue, which would lead me to the 10 freeway. If you've ever driven on this part of La Brea Avenue, the cars can get fairly close to each other. As I was driving along - in "civilian clothes" - I noticed that the car in the lane to my left was tracking exactly with me for a little while. I didn't look over until the driver tapped on their horn. I glanced over to see an SUV with excited kids who had their faces against the windows - smiling and waving wildly. I smiled and waved back, which excited all of them even more. I grabbed some candy canes out of the stocking, and when we stopped at the next light I rolled down my window, showed them to the adult in the front passenger seat and mouthed, "Is this ok?" She nodded "Yes!" and rolled down her window so I could hand them off to her. Again, the cars are pretty close to each other, so this was fairly easy to do without any danger or laws being broken. I heard the squeals of excitement through her open window, and a chorus of "Thank you Santa!!" from the back seats. I waved and said, "Merry Christmas!" I rolled up my window and continued as the light turned green. They turned left, and I smiled thinking about how fun that was. A couple of lights later, I heard another tap on a car horn. I thought, "Are they back?" and I looked to my left. This time, I saw a car full of twenty-somethings waving at me. One of them had their window down and shouted, "Can we have candy canes too Santa?!" I grabbed some more candy canes and we did another hand off. This proceeded for the next three lights as different cars with people of all types pulled up next to me. Just spreading Christmas cheer one car at a time.

REFLECTION:

Life has its daily ups and downs, and that can be especially felt at Christmas time. It's amazing how a random gesture like giving someone a candy cane, or paying for the meal of the person behind you at the drive thru can bring a moment of joy into someone's day.

- Have you ever done or received a random gesture that brought a little joy into an ordinary day?

Dec. 15ᵗʰ

"The human race has one really effective weapon, and that's laughter."

– Mark Twain.

And now, some funny tidbits from a few of my encounters!

That moment when you're trying to maintain eye contact with the 5-year-old boy who's come to visit Santa, but you're distracted by his right nostril and the rhythmic, pulsating in and out movement of a snot bubble.

I had a visit with a little guy named Lucas. He was very animated while talking to me. For those of you who speak "3-year-old", you'll understand what he said to me when I asked him what he wanted for Christmas. Lucas said, "I had...the wewy beh twanfommuh..wike dis (hand gestures, wide eyes) i wan the pah padoh...then the whoaaa...and then weggos...ok."

Quote of the day: At the shopping center I appear at often, we hand out marshmallow treats to the kids. This morning when I handed one to a 7-year-old boy after we took pictures. He took it and asked me very sincerely - "Is it vegan?" Only in L.A.

A sweet looking older lady wanted to have her picture taken with her grandson. She sat down next to me, and immediately placed her hand on my thigh. She said, "Hellooooo Santa!" Her daughter was standing next to the photographer and said, "Mom! There is a Mrs. Claus ya' know!" Grandmom replied, "Mrs. Claus ain't here!"

One night I visited the home of a Labradoodle breeder. If families wanted to, they could include the adorable puppies in their pictures. A family with three boys arrived and wanted to use the puppies. While I was posing with the boys - and all of us were holding puppies - I had a quick, quiet exchange with the oldest boy of around 10 years old. He made a face and quietly said, "Ew. This puppy just tooted." I said to him, "Ya' know, blaming the dog for that never works. Trust me." He burst out laughing which made me laugh too. The mom asked, "What are you two laughing at?' At the same time, we both quickly answered "Nothing!" I then said, "Everyone say smelly cheese!" We both burst out laughing again as the picture was taken.

I was at Walmart and standing in one of the main aisles when a little boy and his mom passed me. The boy did a double take at me, his mouth dropped open and he kept staring at me as they walked by mouth open the whole time. I waved to him, and he continued to look back at me with his mouth open as he walked away. He didn't see the display in the middle of the aisle that he was walking towards. I said, "Hey Buddy. Watch where you're going." I guess he didn't hear me because he walked right into it. He was ok, and a good sport. I helped him up and he said, "Thank you Santa." As he and his mom walked away I heard him say, "Mom, Santa shops here?"

I had an appearance in L.A. and needed to use my GPS. It sent me to the wrong location. What a surprise! I ended up pulling into a driveway at Universal Studios - going the wrong way. A very military looking security guard yelled, "Stop your car!" I stopped and rolled down the driver's side window to wait for him to come over. He approached yelling at me. Then, when he saw me in my Santa regalia he abruptly stopped yelling and stood there with his mouth open. I said, "I'm really sorry. I'm lost and looking for (gave the address)." He went back to his "security mode" and said, "Do you realize that you are going the wrong way?!" I said, "Yes sir. And I'm very sorry. What can I do to help fix this?" He said, "Do you realize this is the entrance for a special Universal Studios event?! What are you trying to pull?" Smiling, I said, "You know Brian, you're on the Nice List right now. Don't blow it." He paused and looked at me. Then in military style he said, "That is very funny sir. Please pull over to the green curb and we will assist you Santa." I said, "Thank you Brian. You'll have a special gift this Christmas." He said, "Merry Christmas, sir." I love it when they play along!

I was driving from one visit to the next, and was still dressed in my Santa suit. As I stopped at a red light, I heard "SANTA!". I looked to my left and there was a carload of teen girls. One of them shouted, "Can we take a selfie with you?!" I said, "A Santa Selfie? Sure!" thinking that when the light changed we'd pull into a parking lot to take the picture. While still at the light, all of the girls suddenly jumped out of their car, ran up to the driver's side window of my car and took the picture. They made it back to her car just as the light was changing. These are all good reminders to not get so caught up in our crazy, busy lives that we miss the little celebrations that pop up every day. Go out and find a moment of fun and laughter in the next 24 hours!

Dec. 16th

"In the end, nothing we do or say in this lifetime will matter as much as the way we have loved one another."

– Daphne Rose Kingma.

I had a wonderful conversation with a girl of around 8 years old. She had a sweet, lovely smile on her face as she came up to have her picture taken with me. She sat next to me, and as we got ready to pose for the picture, she looked up at me. The look in her eyes was the one that made you realize how important Santa is in the life of this child and many others. It's that look of "I believe in you with all of my heart." She hugged me with both arms, and as we posed she laid her head on my shoulder. After the picture, we started talking and she continued to look directly in my eyes with that same look. Our conversation took on a rather relaxed, comfortable feeling as she started telling me about what she'd done so far on her vacation. I just listened and let her talk and she seemed very happy to be able to tell me these things. Then she asked me about the Naughty and Nice List. "What kinds of things can get someone put on THAT list?" "What can they do to get off of it, and is it hard to put someone on the Naughty List?" (Smart, articulate girl for her age!) Her parents seemed to be wanting to go, but I asked if it was ok if I answered her question about "The List"! They said it was ok, so I asked her why she was so interested in the lists. She paused and I told her that she didn't have to answer that question if she didn't feel comfortable doing that. She looked me directly in the eyes for a few seconds and then smiled. I asked, "What?" She replied, "I can tell by looking in your sparkly eyes that I can trust you." I didn't know what to say, but she saved me by telling me why she was asking. She said, "My cousin Bella picks on me a lot." "I'm sorry" I replied. She went on to tell me that she doesn't know why Bella treats her that way, and that it really hurts her feelings. I asked her if Bella had always acted that way towards her, and she said, "No. We've always been like sisters." Her dad said, "Time to go!" She looked at me as if to say, "Can I please keep talking to you?" I smiled at her parents and said, "Five more minutes? Pretty please? You have a wonderful daughter and I'd like to be able to answer her question." Dad started to say something, but Mom stopped him and shook her head "Yes".

I looked back at her and saw that she was still looking directly at me. I said to her, "Have you told Bella how it makes you feel?" She said "Yes, but it didn't seem to do any good." I looked right at her and said, "My dear, sometimes people are going through their own difficult times in life. They're stressed out about something or they just might not be very happy with themselves. So, instead of trying to do something positive about their problems, they lash out at someone else. It happens to everyone...not just Bella. Do you understand that?" "Yes Santa". "Ok" I said. "Now here's the truth. Deep down inside, Bella loves you. She's probably as confused as you are about why she's acting that way. So, the best thing that you can do is to love her. Showing love to another person can do amazing things. And I can tell that you're a young lady that has a lot of love in her heart for everyone. Does that make sense?" "Yes, it does Santa," she replied. "I'm going to do the best that I can for Bella." I took her by the hand and said, "That's all you need to do honey, is the best that you can." Then she asked me, "Can I come back and talk to you again sometime?" I replied, "You can come talk to me any time that you and your family are in this area and I'm visiting here too. You can come back here and talk to me about anything. I'll always have time for you." She hugged me and said, "I love you Santa. Thank you." I said, "Santa loves you too sweetheart." She got up and joined her parents and they left. As they walked away, she kept turning around to look at me and smile. And just before they turned the corner to go out of sight, she turned around once more, smiled and waved.

REFLECTION:

As parents, it hurts when your child is being bullied by a classmate or family member. You want to step in and fix it yourselves because it's your job to protect your child.

- What can you do to help your child to be an example of friendship and love to the person mistreating them, while also lifting them up and encouraging them?

Dec. 17th

"Sometimes the questions are complicated and the answers are simple."

— Dr. Seuss.

I was leaving the hospital yesterday after visiting with someone and I needed to make some phone calls before I hit the road. Lost in my thoughts, I sat down in the waiting area across from the Outpatient Diagnostic Center. A few minutes after I sat down, I heard a female-mom-voice saying, "Gabriel. Come back here!" A little African-American boy of around 7-8 years old plopped into the chair next to me. I glanced over at him and said, "Hey". He said hey back and I continued to check the notes that I had written down for my phone calls. In my peripheral vision, I could see that he was still looking at me. I stopped what I was doing to talk to him as his mom approached. She said, "I'm sorry. He said that he wanted to ask you something." I replied, "It's ok. So Gabriel, what's on your mind?" Both Gabriel and Mom looked surprised that I knew his name. Gabriel then said, "Mom. Can you give us some privacy?" (I like this kid already) Mom was cool about it and said, "Ok honey. I'll be right over here." She walked out of earshot and sat down. He looked back at me and I asked, "What can I do for you my friend?" He said, "I need some answers that no one else will tell me." I replied, "Answers about what?" With a very serious look on his face he said, "My granddad is in that room back there." He pointed to the Diagnostic Area. "I asked my mom why we were here" he continued. "But all she said was 'Oh, Granddad is just having a check up'." I looked at him and said, "But you think there's more to it than that, right?". "Right" he said. "Well, what makes you think there's more to it?" I asked. He shifted in his seat to turn and look at me and said, "Because I've heard mama on the phone talking about Granddad, and she's said the word cancer. Cancer isn't good." I paused and then looked him in the eyes and said, "No Gabriel, it's not. Cancer sucks." He looked surprised and said, "Santa! You said sucks!" I said, "Yes I did. Sorry. Now then, that room back there is for doing tests and finding out what might be wrong with someone. I want you to focus on the fact I said, 'Might be wrong with someone'. You see, they do all of these tests to find out what's wrong with someone like your granddad, or to find out if there isn't anything serious – like cancer – that's wrong with someone." He pondered on that for a minute and then said, "So granddad might not have cancer?" I said, "That's right. He might not. But if he does there are a ton of things that can be done to make him better. Now, I know that this whole thing seems huge, but there is one thing you can do to help your granddad. With any illness, it's important to stay positive and laugh as often as you can. Do you know what makes your granddad laugh?" He smiled and said, "Kevin Hart". I laughed and said, "Ok. Kevin Hart is funny. But there's also what makes him happy. And I'll bet when you're happy, he's happy. Right?" With a shy smile he said, "Yeah." I said, "Now I don't want you to feel that there's any pressure on you. You just keep being your granddad's buddy and things will be fine. He loves you more than anything and he's very, very proud of the young man you're becoming." Wide-eyed, he looked at me and asked, "How do you know that?" I smiled and said, "Santa knows stuff like that." We both heard a loud sniffle and looked over at his mom. She was wiping her eyes. Gabriel looked at me and said, "Why do moms do that?" I tried not to laugh and said, "Because moms feel things differently than us guys. That's what makes them great. Are we good my man?" He smiled and said, "Yep. Thanks Santa." "Anytime" I replied. I stood up to leave and his mom walked over and said, "I just...you are...thank you." "My pleasure" I said. I left quickly because I was starting to get choked up.

REFLECTIONS:
Sometimes kids understand more than we give them credit for understanding. Most of the time if we try to deflect their questions with our response or answer, they'll see right through them. Kids are smart!

- What are some good ways to handle it when a child asks honest, direct questions? (This question is for adults and kids)

Dec. 18th

"We worry about what a child will become tomorrow, yet we forget that he is someone today."

– Stacia Tauscher.

There were two little boys who were brothers who came to have their Christmas pictures done. Both of them were under 8 years old and their dad accompanied them. The older brother came up first and we had a great conversation while Dad enthusiastically took pictures. Next, the little brother came up. He wasn't as enthusiastic as his big brother, but not afraid to come see Santa. I said, "How cool is this? I'm here visiting for the day because I love coming to this place, and look at this! I get to see you! Bonus!" He smiled a very sweet smile and I told him that I knew that it was early, but did he have any ideas about what he wanted for Christmas? He held my gaze for a few seconds, and then looked away and then down at his hands that were folded on his lap. I looked down at his little hands as he started to wring them nervously. I then said, "Well, why don't we start by talking about some of the stuff you like? I'll bet you like remote control cars." Without looking up, he nodded his head "yes". His dad chimed in, "What's up buddy? Are you afraid Santa knows that you've been a bad boy?" I looked over at the dad, who had an "I'm having fun giving my kid a hard time" grin on his face. Without looking at me, this little guy said, "Santa...I've been bad. I've done bad stuff." My heart started breaking. I said, "Hey buddy. Look at me. Please? It's ok." He looked up at me with tears welling. I looked him in the eyes - my own tears welling up - and said, "So what? You made a mistake. I make mistakes all the time. Just ask Mrs. Claus! It's ok if you mess up or make a wrong choice as long as you learn from it and try your hardest not to do it again. I've made a ton of mistakes, but I know that Mrs. Claus still loves me. And so do your family and friends. I really mean that! Ya' gotta trust Santa on this one. And I love you too buddy!" He said, "Thank you Santa." and hugged me. As he was leaving, I looked at Dad and by the look on his face I think he got the message. I smiled at him because I wanted him to know that I realize dads make mistakes too, and we need to learn from them as well.

REFLECTION:
Two things never change about children. A child's earnest need to have the approval of their parents, and know that they're good and their parents are proud of them no matter what. The other thing that never changes is a child's heart. It is just as fragile and susceptible to hurt, as was the heart of the child that Christmas is all about.

-       What can you do to encourage someone who has made a mistake, rather than make them feel bad about it?

Dec. 19th

"Great opportunities to help others seldom come, but small ones surround us every day."

– Sally Koch.

There's a verse in the book of Hebrews in the Bible that says, "Don't forget to show hospitality to strangers, for some who have done this have entertained angels without realizing it!" Well, I may have had an "angel" come to visit me once while I was appearing at a place for Santa photos. Just one disclaimer – this is not a Santa or Christmas type story. But it's a great story, so I hope you'll keep reading. My "angel's" name is straight out of Mayberry - RJ Calhoun. He was an older man with a very kind face and a calm, pleasant demeanor. He was casually dressed in a baseball cap, a beige windbreaker, a slightly darker colored golf shirt buttoned all the way up, khakis and white tennis shoes. He reminded me of how George Burns dressed in the movie, "Oh, God". RJ proceeded to tell me about a friend of his who is a missionary in South America. You see, RJ and his friend are involved with a non-profit organization that translates Bibles into many different languages and then distributes them. RJ's friend became acquainted with a man in a village by the name of Barnaby. He described Barnaby as a somewhat lazy man, who pretty much liked to just sit around and smoke. He didn't have enough money to afford actual cigarettes, so he bought tobacco and would wrap it in anything he could find in order to smoke it. On one visit, RJ's friend found Barnaby and told him that he wanted to give him a copy of the New Testament that was translated into his own native language. Barnaby told the man that he appreciated the offer, but to be honest - he probably would end up tearing out the pages and using them to smoke. So, he refused the Bible because he didn't feel right about doing that. BJ's friend thought for a moment and then told Barnaby, "I'll make you a deal. I'll give you this New Testament as long as you promise me that you'll read each page before you tear it out and use it for smoking." Barnaby pondered this offer, and then agreed. After this, RJ's friend took some time off - as missionaries who spend a great deal of time in the field need to do. He returned home for a month or so to rejuvenate. Then he went back to that same village in South America. Immediately he began looking for Barnaby, but he was nowhere to be found. He asked around everywhere that he could think of, but the answer was the same. No one knew where Barnaby was. More to come tomorrow!

REFLECTION:

It's not easy to talk with some people about religion. Being a missionary in a foreign country is a brave and challenging calling, that a lot of people wouldn't even consider doing with their life. I have tremendous respect for anyone deciding to enter this field.

-       Is the deal that RJ's friend made for giving Barnaby the New Testament a good example of serving others?

Dec. 20th

"What wisdom can you find that is greater than kindness?"

– Jean-Jacques Rousseau.

SPOILER ALERT: If you didn't read yesterday's story, before you go any further let me encourage you to go back and read it before reading this one. Picking up where we left off - Barnaby was missing. RJ told me that his missionary friend had searched everywhere for him, but with no luck. He began to wonder if he'd done the right thing. Had he been Barnaby's enabler in continuing his extreme smoking habit and lazy lifestyle? As he pondered this thought, he went to a meeting in a nearby town. He found a seat in the crowded tent and looked around at the crowd. He looked up towards the speaker's platform and couldn't believe what he saw. It was Barnaby! At that same moment, Barnaby's eyes met his startled friend's gaze. Barnaby quickly made his way to his friend who said, "Barnaby! I've been looking everywhere for you! What are you doing here? What...what's going on?". Barnaby said, "Do you remember that copy of the New Testament that you gave me?" "Of course I do." he replied. Barnaby continued. "I did what you asked of me. I read Matthew...and I smoked Matthew." Slightly disappointed the man said, "Oh. Ok." "And then..." Barnaby said. I read Mark. Then I smoked Mark!" RJ's friend thought "This is going from bad to worse!". "The same thing with Luke" said Barnaby. "And then I started with John. And I came to a verse that caused me to stop. Stopped me dead in my tracks." RJ asked me, "Do you know what verse that was?" I said, "My guess would be John 3:16." "That's right" said RJ. "For God so loved the world, that he gave his one and only Son, that whoever believes in Him shall not perish but have eternal life." Barnaby went on to explain that out of everything he had read, this is the one thing that affected him the most. How could he even think of tearing out a page that contained those words on them - let alone smoke it? As a matter of fact, he stopped smoking at that very moment and never smoked again. And he was at that meeting to share his story and what God had done in his life. RJ's missionary friend was thankful that his gesture of giving Barnaby a copy of the New Testament made a difference. But he knew that he was just the conduit for exposing such powerful words to a man from a remote village - and it changed his life. "You see" RJ said to me with his eyes twinkling, "You never know how the smallest gesture of kindness can affect someone who least expects it...or thinks they need it." At that moment, a small child and her parents came around the corner, and the little girl exclaimed "Santa!" I looked at RJ to ask him to please wait. Before I could, he said, "You're on Santa!" So, I went over to spend some time with the little girl and her parents. When I finished, I looked around for RJ - but he was gone.

REFLECTION:
My encounter with this unassuming man made such an impact on me. The story that he shared with me was exactly what I needed to hear at that moment.

- When has a kind gesture from someone else, or one that you have done, made a great impact?

Dec. 21st

"It is not our differences that divide us. It is our inability to recognize, accept and celebrate those differences"

– Anonymous.

As I was walking to the area where I was to do Santa photos, I passed a family of a mom and dad, and a boy and girl around 8-10 years old. The parents waved, and the kids stopped and stared with their mouths open. I reached out and hi-fived both of the kids - but neither one of them said anything. I got settled inside the photo and proceeded to see some families. At this particular location, you don't have to only get your picture taken to see Santa. If you want to, you can just walk through and say hi. After around 30 minutes of visiting with families and taking pictures, the family that I saw on my way there came in just to say hi. The kids came up and hugged me and I asked them what they wanted for Christmas. The kids looked back at their parents, then looked back at me. The girl said, "We don't celebrate Christmas." I said, "Ok. That's just fine. I'm just very happy that I got to say hi to you." The dad stepped forward and said, "Santa, we are Jewish and celebrate Hanukkah." I replied, "Well I think that's wonderful." The dad continued, "After we saw you earlier, my children asked if it was ok to come and see you. They've never asked that about Santa before. I asked why and they said, 'Because he's the real one.' So, we said yes." At first, I didn't know what to say, but I looked at the two kids - who had looks on their faces as if to say, "I hope this is ok!" I reached out and took their hands and said, "I am honored that you wanted to come and see me." I started to tear up, and the boy asked "Santa? Are you ok?" I said, "Yes, I'm ok. It's just that this really means a lot to me. Your whole family is such a great example of love and acceptance. Thank you so much for coming to see me." I got another hug from the kids, mom patted me on the shoulder. Then Dad and I exchanged a very warm two-handed handshake. I said, "Thank you very much. And Happy Hanukkah." He said, "Thank YOU Santa. And Merry Christmas!"

REFLECTION:

That was a very special moment. During the holiday season when people celebrate it in different ways, this family – by the example of the parents – chose to show acceptance of differing beliefs instead of putting up walls that could resonate in other aspects of their children's lives.

-        Have you ever faced a similar situation, and how did you handle it?

Dec. 22nd

"I feel the capacity to care is the thing which gives life its deepest significance."

– Pablo Casals.

I was at the store today picking up a few things that were on "The List" that my wife gave me. I put that in quotes because most husbands know that when your wife gives you "The List", you do NOT get anything that isn't on it. So, I'm concentrating and trying not to get distracted - when I feel a light tug on the back of my shirt. I turned my head expecting to be somewhat eye-to-eye with whoever did that, but all I saw were the items on the shelves across the aisle. I was puzzled for a few seconds until I heard a tiny voice say, "Hi!" I looked down and saw a girl that was around 7 years old looking up at me. "Well hello there sweetheart" I said. She looked me right in the eyes and said in a very direct tone, "You're Santa, huh?" I smiled at her and glanced up at her mom, who said, "I'm sorry." I told the mom that it was ok and knelt down on one knee to talk to her. "Well young lady, let's keep that Santa thing between the two of us for right now?" She said, "Of course. But can I ask you something?" "You can ask me anything you want", I replied. She turned to look at her mom and said, "Mommy, can you give us a minute?" I was trying not to laugh when I looked at the mom, and she smiled and said "Ok honey. I'll be right down here." And with that, the mom went to the end of the aisle. By the look this little girl gave me next, I could tell she was ready to get down to business. "What can I do for you?" I asked. " She said, "This isn't for me, it's for my mommy. She hasn't been very happy lately because of stuff going on that she won't tell me about." I said, "Well honey, it's not because your mommy doesn't trust you or anything like that. It's because she loves you so much that she wants to protect you and take care of things like parents are supposed to do. Now, you seem to be a very smart and caring young lady..." - the young lady's comment got a big, proud smile from her - "...and I know that because you notice that your mommy has a lot on her mind." "That's what I mean!" she replied. "I know she's thinking about a lot of stuff and I think that's what's making her unhappy. Can you please use your Santa magic and make her happy again?" I looked her in the eyes and said, "Here's what I can do. I'm going to make you an honorary elf." She gasped. I continued, "Now then, take both of your hands and grab hold of your ears." She complied. I then said, "Now repeat after me. I promise to uphold all of the duties of being an honorary elf." She repeated what I said. "And my special task will be to love my mommy and help her with anything that is in my power to do." I paused and said, "You know what? That was a lot to repeat, so just say 'I will'". "I will!" she said. I said, "Congratulations. You're an honorary elf. Now then, about what you asked me about before. Your mommy doesn't need to tell you everything that she's thinking about. You don't tell her everything you're thinking about, do you?" She answered, "Well...no. But what are you going to do to help my mommy?" I said, "I just did it. YOU are your mother's guardian elf. And all that means is to always love her, trust her and be the best daughter that you can be. That will ALWAYS make your mommy happy no matter what. I know you can do it because I've already seen you do it. That's why you're on the Nice List!" "I am?!" she said. "Of course you are. Now guardian elf...get to work." I took her by the hand and we walked over to where her mom was. "She's quite a girl" I said to the mom. She thanked me for talking to her daughter, and as I walked away I turned, looked at the girl and grabbed both of my ears. The girl did the same and giggled.

REFLECTION:
The definition of caring is "a feeling of being concerned for someone and having an urge to show kindness to them." This little girl was such a great example of caring. She noticed something about her mother, and instead of giving up when she didn't know what to do - she shared what was on her heart.
-      Is it difficult to share your concerns with someone else when you can't find the answer on your own?

Dec. 23ʳᵈ

"Keep your families close and love and honor your children."

– Gordon B. Hinckley.

As the large family entered the Santa photo area and began to assemble for their photo, they seemed quiet amongst all of the Christmas commotion going on around them. Almost stoic. Everyone began taking their places around the Santa chair without much need for direction from the photographer. I moved to the far right of the chair, and a young boy of around 8 years old sat on my immediate left and a 12-year-old girl sat next to him. The boy was holding a stuffed toy, and before I had the chance to say anything to the kids, their mom appeared in front of me holding a framed photo of a baby. She said, "This is a picture of our baby boy, who passed away a few months ago." She handed the picture frame to the girl, who was bravely trying not to cry, but had a tear running down her right cheek. I suddenly realized she was the older sister of the baby boy. The mom reached out and gently touched the stuffed animal and said, "This has our baby's heartbeat recorded on it. Would you mind holding it along with his brother?" With emotion straining her voice she continued. "You see, our baby boy didn't get to have his first photo with Santa, so we're all gathered here to make that happen." I could barely get out, "It would be my honor." I looked in the direction of the camera, but was having trouble seeing it clearly. I heard sniffing coming from behind the photographer and noticed the family waiting in line to have their picture taken next. It was obvious that they realized what was going on in the room, wiping tears away. My right hand held the stuffed toy along with my brother, and with my left arm draped across his and the sister's shoulders - I did my best to try and comfort them. With love and honor, this wonderful family of a mom and dad, brother and sister, aunts, uncles and grandparents all had their Christmas pictures taken...along with their precious baby boy. After they were finished, I hugged the kids for a long time. The mom patted my shoulder and I looked up at her and said, "Thank you so much for letting me be a part of this with your family." Without needing to say anything, the photographer and the family that was next in line took a few minutes to gather our composure.

REFLECTION:

I have been a part of many, many "Baby's First Santa Pictures". But I will never forget this special moment.The emotions that you feel from the loss of a loved one are especially magnified during that first Christmas without them. Try to think of the happy, joyful memories that you experienced with them. And remember, you're not alone.

Dec. 24th

"Everyone is precious. Everyone matters".

– Archbishop Desmond Tutu.

It's Christmas Eve! The energy and excitement of the season were definitely in high gear all day. Kids AND adults having their own Buddy the Elf - "SANTAAAA!!!" - moments and the visits with both age groups ran the gamut of emotions. I was finished taking pictures at 4 pm and could not wait to get on the road because I had a long trip ahead of me. As I was getting into the car in the parking lot, I noticed a mom helping her little boy into his car seat. I didn't want the boy to see Santa in my "traveling clothes" at this point on Christmas Eve. So, I stayed out of sight until she was finished strapping him in and was walking over to the driver's side of her car. I quickly got into my car and had just started the engine when I was startled by a knock on the window. I looked over and there was the mom that had helped the little boy in the car. She had a very excited look on her face and motioned for me to roll down the window. I did, and she asked me if I could "pleeeeeaaase" come to say hi to her son. For a brief moment, I considered saying "I'm sorry. I really need to get going." But I looked from her face that said, "I really need for this to happen." - to see her little guy's brown hair barely visible in the car window...and I did what Santa would do. I got out of the car and went over to grant one last Christmas Wish for this season. The mom opened the door and said, "Honey! It's Santa!". Any concern that I had with him wondering what Santa was doing there and dressed the way I was, vanished immediately with the sweet look of surprise and joy in his eyes. What mattered was the fact that he was getting a private visit from Santa. I glanced around the car and noticed that it looked like everything they owned was in there. I knew then that I'd made the right choice. I told him that I was on my way to the North Pole right now to start my deliveries, but I just had to stop and say hi to my special friend. He said, "I'm your special friend?" I replied, "Of course you are!" Excitedly he said, "Mommy, did you hear that? I'm Santa's special friend!!" Mommy was too busy jumping up and down and clapping her hands to reply. We talked for a few more minutes. He had a lot of questions about the reindeer, how I was going to deliver everything to everyone around the world, and the current location of my sleigh. I answered all of his questions, and then told him it was time for me to go. He gave me a big hug and said, "Best Christmas gift EVER!!" As I turned to go back to my car, the mom said, "I don't know what to say." I told her Merry Christmas, and she hugged me and I left them both talking excitedly to each other about what just happened.

REFLECTION:
This was the perfect end to the Christmas season. Sometimes we can be in such a rush, that we miss giving our attention to someone else who could really use it. But I'm very thankful that I stopped and took the time with this little guy. His mom was hoping for a small Christmas miracle for her son, and she made it happen.

-       When was the last time you were very busy, but still took the time for someone else?

Dec. 25th

"Promise me you'll always remember: you're braver than you believe, stronger than you seem, and smarter than you think."

– Winnie The Pooh.

Santa isn't always finished after visiting the last house on Christmas morning. I had one last stop to visit and deliver presents to some sweet and brave kids at a Children's Hospital. They didn't know Santa was coming, and the looks on the faces of the children and family members were very heart warming. Each child's room was decorated simply and warmly. Small Christmas trees with lights and adorned with lovingly crafted homemade ornaments. Displays of cards – store bought and handmade - either on the window sills, or hung with string on the wall. In a few rooms, there was Christmas music playing softly amid the beeps and sounds of hospital equipment. There were many wonderful experiences. One little boy had one question after another for me. He started with, "Where's your sleigh?" I answered, "In a secret place. "He followed quickly with, "Am I on The Nice List?" I smiled and said, "Well of course you are! You've been on there every year!" That got a huge smile. He then asked," Which one is your favorite reindeer?" I replied, "I don't really have a favorite. Although there is one that used to cause a little trouble." He looked surprised and asked, "Which one?" I said, "Olive." He looked at me as if to say "Who?" I said, "You know...Olive, the other reindeer. Used to laugh and call him names." He paused for a second and then laughed and said, "Good one Santa." Then there was the sweet moment when a 6-year-old girl patient softly sang "Santa Claus Is Coming To Town" to me. I told her that it was the most beautiful version of that song I'd ever heard. She smiled the most precious smile. My final visits were in the NICU, or the neonatal intensive care unit. As I quietly went about placing the teddy bears by each baby, I heard someone softly singing. I rounded a corner and came upon a granddaddy sitting alone by a crib, holding his tiny new grandson while rocking him and quietly singing "Away In A Manger". His back was to me, so I didn't disturb their special time together. I just left the gift for the baby on a small table next to the open crib.

REFLECTION:
After leaving the hospital, I drove in silence for a while. I wasn't sure what to expect for this visit. Christmas mornings are traditionally very active with lots of excitement. But the quietness I experienced wasn't somber or heavy. It was peaceful. I came away feeling so blessed to be able to share a very special Christmas morning with the kids, families and the amazing nurses who take care of - and love on - these wonderful children. Merry Christmas!

-     Share your favorite Christmas morning memories.

Epilogue

Being Santa Claus is much more than putting on the red suit and saying "Ho-ho-ho!". People of all ages will share with Santa not only what they want for Christmas, but what is on their hearts. And that runs the gamut of a brother is picking on them, to family issues, illnesses and life-changing decisions. When a child looks at you with eyes that are saying, "I believe in you!", or an adult's eyes that say, "I just need someone to talk to.", you take on that responsibility to the best of your abilities and pray for the right words to say to them. Everyone who comes to see Santa should walk away happy. Every child should know that Santa is always there for them and is their best friend no matter what. That's why no matter if I encounter a child while in my Santa suit or in "civilian clothes", I will do my best to Always Be Santa.

Merry Christmas!

Made in the USA
Coppell, TX
25 October 2024

39168587R00040